T0275407

GRIFFIN POETRY PRIZE
Anthology 2024

Published in Canada and the USA in 2024 by House of Anansi Press Inc.
houseofanansi.com

House of Anansi Press is a Global Certified Accessible™ (GCA by Benetech) publisher.
The ebook version of this book meets stringent accessibility standards and is available to
readers with print disabilities.

28 27 26 25 24   1 2 3 4 5

Library and Archives Canada Cataloguing in Publication

Cataloguing data available from Library and Archives Canada

Cover design: Kyra Griffin and Chloé Griffin
Cover artwork: Simone Gilges; *Planet im Nebel I*, 2016; Silver gelatin print, carbon toner.
Interior cover artwork: Constantin Brancusi (1876–1957). *Sleeping Muse*, 1910. © Succession
Brancusi - All rights reserved (ADAGP) / CARCC Ottawa 2024. Bronze, 6¾ x 9½ x 6 in. (17.1 x
24.1 x 15.2 cm); Weight: 12 lbs. Alfred Stieglitz Collection, 1949 (49.70.225). The Metropolitan
Museum of Art, New York, NY, USA. Photo Credit: Image copyright © The Metropolitan
Museum of Art. Image source: Art Resource, NY.

*House of Anansi Press is grateful for the privilege to work on and create from the Traditional Territory
of many Nations, including the Anishinabeg, the Wendat, and the Haudenosaunee, as well as the
Treaty Lands of the Mississaugas of the Credit.*

**Canada Council
for the Arts**

**Conseil des Arts
du Canada**

ONTARIO ARTS COUNCIL
CONSEIL DES ARTS DE L'ONTARIO
an Ontario government agency
un organisme du gouvernement de l'Ontario

With the participation of the Government of Canada
Avec la participation du gouvernement du Canada | **Canada**

*We acknowledge for their financial support of our publishing program the Canada Council
for the Arts, the Ontario Arts Council, and the Government of Canada.*

Printed and bound in Canada

GRIFFIN POETRY PRIZE
Anthology 2024

A SELECTION OF THE SHORTLIST

Edited by ALBERT F. MORITZ

2001

International
Yehuda Amichai
    Translated by Chana Bloch and
    Chana Kronfeld
Paul Celan
    Translated by Nikolai Popov
    and Heather McHugh
Fanny Howe
Les Murray

Canadian
Anne Carson
Ghandl of the Qayahl Llaanas
    Translated by Robert
    Bringhurst
Don McKay

2002

International
Victor Hernández Cruz
Christopher Logue
Les Murray
Alice Notley

Canadian
Christian Bök
Erín Moure
Karen Solie

2003

International
Kathleen Jamie
Paul Muldoon
Gerald Stern
C. D. Wright

Canadian
Margaret Avison
Dionne Brand
P. K. Page

2004

International
Suji Kwock Kim
David Kirby
August Kleinzahler
Louis Simpson

Canadian
Di Brandt
Leslie Greentree
Anne Simpson

2005

International	Canadian
Fanny Howe	**Roo Borson**
Michael Symmons Roberts	George Bowering
Matthew Rohrer	Don McKay
Charles Simic	

2006

International	Canadian
Kamau Brathwaite	Phil Hall
Durs Grünbein	**Sylvia Legris**
Translated by Michael	Erín Moure
Hofmann	
Michael Palmer	
Dunya Mikhail	
Translated by Elizabeth Winslow	

2007

International	Canadian
Paul Farley	Ken Babstock
Rodney Jones	**Don McKay**
Frederick Seidel	Priscila Uppal
Charles Wright	

2008

International	Canadian
John Ashbery	**Robin Blaser**
Elaine Equi	Nicole Brossard
César Vallejo	Translated by Robert Majzels
Translated by Clayton	and Erín Moure
Eshleman	David W. McFadden
David Harsent	

2009

International	Canadian
Mick Imlah	Kevin Connolly
Derek Mahon	Jeramy Dodds
C. D. Wright	**A. F. Moritz**
Dean Young	

2010

International	*Canadian*
John Glenday	Kate Hall
Louise Glück	P. K. Page
Eiléan Ní Chuilleanáin	**Karen Solie**
Valérie Rouzeau	
Translated by Susan Wicks	

2011

International	*Canadian*
Seamus Heaney	**Dionne Brand**
Adonis	Suzanne Buffam
Translated by Khaled Mattawa	John Steffler
François Jacqmin	
Translated by Philip Mosley	
Gjertrud Schnackenberg	

2012

International	*Canadian*
David Harsent	**Ken Babstock**
Yusef Komunyakaa	Phil Hall
Sean O'Brien	Jan Zwicky
Tadeusz Różewicz	
Translated by Joanna Trzeciak	

2013

International	*Canadian*
Ghassan Zaqtan	**David W. McFadden**
Translated by Fady Joudah	James Pollock
Jennifer Maiden	Ian Williams
Alan Shapiro	
Brenda Shaughnessy	

2014

International	*Canadian*
Rachael Boast	**Anne Carson**
Brenda Hillman	Sue Goyette
Carl Phillips	Anne Michaels
Tomasz Różycki	
Translated by Mira Rosenthal	

2015

International
Wang Xiaoni
   Translated by Eleanor Goodman
Wioletta Grzegorzewska
   Translated by Marek
   Kazmierski
Michael Longley
Spencer Reece

Canadian
Shane Book
Jane Munro
Russell Thornton

2016

International
Norman Dubie
Joy Harjo
Don Paterson
Rowan Ricardo Phillips

Canadian
Ulrikka S. Gernes
   Translated by Per Brask and
   Patrick Friesen
Liz Howard
Soraya Peerbaye

2017

International
Jane Mead
Abdellatif Laâbi
   Translated by Donald
   Nicholson-Smith
Alice Oswald
Denise Riley

Canadian
Jordan Abel
Hoa Nguyen
Sandra Ridley

2018

International
Tongo Eisen-Martin
Susan Howe
Layli Long Soldier
Natalie Shapero

Canadian
Billy-Ray Belcourt
Aisha Sasha John
Donato Mancini

2019

International
Raymond Antrobus
Daniel Borzutzky
Kim Hyesoon
    Translated by Don Mee Choi
Luljeta Lleshanaku
    Translated by Ani Gjika

Canadian
Dionne Brand
Eve Joseph
Sarah Tolmie

2020

International
Abigail Chabitnoy
Sharon Olds
Etel Adnan
    Translated by Sarah Riggs
Natalie Scenters-Zapico

Canadian
Chantal Gibson
Doyali Farah Islam
Kaie Kellough

2021

International
Victoria Chang
Valzhyna Mort
Srikanth Reddy
Yi Lei
    Translated by Tracy K. Smith
    and Changtai Bi

Canadian
Joseph Dandurand
Canisia Lubrin
Yusuf Saadi

2022

International
Gemma Gorga
    Translated by Sharon Dolin
Douglas Kearney
Natalka Bilotserkivets
    Translated by Ali Kinsella and
    Dzvinia Orlowsky
Ed Roberson

Canadian
David Bradford
Liz Howard
Tolu Oloruntoba

Between 2001 and 2022, the Griffin Poetry Prize was awarded in two categories—Canadian and International—with the total number of submissions received split approximately 50/50. In 2023, the prizes were combined into one major prize to emphasize the international nature of poetry, transcending all borders and languages.

2023

Iman Mersal
    Translated by Robyn Creswell
Ada Limón

Susan Musgrave
Roger Reeves
Ocean Vuong

CONTENTS

PREFACE

Halyna Kruk and her translators, Amelia M. Glaser and Yuliya
Ilchuk, from embattled Ukraine and from a safer but stressed North
America, sing,

> i love you from all the places.
> there's still a lot of uncharted territory,
> you can go on and on …

The poetry of 2023 answered openly to our moment. A keynote was
the current intensification of the modern thrust for freedom in, for
instance, the situations of emigrants, immigrants, and diasporic com-
munities; the continuing effects of colonialism and the recognition of
shifty modes of imperialism; the experience of victims of war and tyr-
anny; the dramas of those disadvantaged and often savaged because
of their difference by rigid political organization and straitjacketing
aspects of cultural history and convention. The COVID-19 pandemic
and its lingering effect, personal and social, must also be mentioned.

These stories are told in many media. Poetry is alone in pre-
senting them through utter uniqueness. Each poem gives us these
dramas through the absolute presence of moments within them
belonging solely to one body, one mind, one soul, one community
(perhaps a microcommunity, e.g., lovers; a mother with a sick child;
an impoverished family in a ramshackle house; a patient and doctor;
a parent with the corpse or the memory of a child …). They belong
to us all by means of being wholly, only themselves, an instant once
and forever.

But the *utter* uniqueness, the uniqueness of the unique, that the poem gives us lies even more deeply in the form of its language, "the form of its flight" (Jiménez). Its exact, unprecedented, inimitable form of language makes *this* poem not just the symbol of a previous moment but the living, transforming prolongation of this moment in the listener. The poets of 2023 fervently grasped this. Ishion Hutchinson:

> He heard the far-off drum of Miriam as he paced with a sharp ringing in his ears among his grandmother's croton plants which glittered like sardius like topaz like diamond like beryl like onyx like jasper like sapphire like emerald like carbuncle like gold like a green ringing green of mildewed croton leaves he would if he could scatter on the turquoise sea.

In the 592 books from 2023, I met good poems everywhere. It would be hard to say how deeply I fell in love with them. Good poems … which do not deal with subject matter by describing, analyzing, evaluating, or championing some approach to it. The poem is not definable as part of any argument or cultural limitation. The poem is pure difference, pure freedom. Arguments and limitations—cultural and otherwise; *all* limitations!—appear in the poem for the same reason that the qualities of stone or scrap appear in a statue. Words, though not limited to concepts, contain concepts and histories, and so these are some of what the poem is made of, like sounds in music and materials in sculpture. So Ann Lauterbach addresses this supplication to us: that we should grasp our most basic freedom, the most necessary of all,

> before war
> before collapse contaminates the real thing the real
> harbor   set sail …

>   speak to us, please,
> be present, be among those

who come forward wearing thin armor   carrying
baskets. Say hello, be gentle and fierce.
Do not fear the past. Bring candor, humor, touch.

While there was a lot of scarification and excoriation in 2023, there
was also a lot of humour, a lot of good humour and joie de vivre
and gusto, and some inimitably mordant closed-lip grins. Also, some
square cold gazes. Very attractive.

Poets addressing of-the-moment issues found the eternal in
them, quest, struggle, peace in achievement, glory even in shipwreck.
Other poets addressed the eternal directly, with a contemporary
form of classic calm and resolve. Each poem brought home to me
that the good poem is, of all human-made things, the one closest to
a human being. We meet it. We converse with it; we lean in, trying
to understand, asking it to repeat itself, bringing other questions. It's
like no other. We believe, we hope, that we are coming nearer. We
know it now … We know what it is, but exactly what it is, we cannot
say. So the hunger comes to meet it again. And when met again, it's
not the same; something new is found; maybe, too, something is lost.
The enchantment of this encounter is not exactly the enchantment
of that one. Jorie Graham:

> are we lost why did
> we just leave
> where we just
>
> were why is
> everything
> so far behind
> now as we go on I
>
> see you think
> when you reach
> me again to ask
> why …

Not everyone will read all these 2023 books of poetry that make contributions of unreproducible humanity in its living moments. The five shortlisted well represent the others and yet cannot represent them. Each of the many deserved to be present. Each is engaged in one of the great efforts of poetry in our age, the rescue of the life of language. The struggle against the reduction of language to technique is especially dire for English, which more than any other tongue is coerced to act as a form of cash and credit, of profitable trivialities, of arrogant rationalism applying itself to the explanation (which means the "flattening out") of all things.

This is one reason why other poetries, translated into a fresh English, are so welcome. They bring us lights that are ours but are hard to see from our own position. Will our world come to seem no more than a diagram of a world that no one any longer touches? Society now strongly tends that way. Or will experience be seen in truth—poetically—as what it is: inexhaustible depth, surprise, lightness, persistence, understanding, possibility? That is poetry's direction: to the side of the light from Homero Aridjis's childhood, the child's light saved and prolonged into our lives in poetry:

I saw you coming down the walls
I saw you bleed under the door
I saw you searching inside for me
I saw you paint the mountains blue
I followed you on the liquid fingers of water
I swaddled you in your transparent body
I embraced you, infinite light intelligent light …

Albert F. Moritz, Toronto, March 2024
The quotations in this preface are drawn from poems not included in the anthology.

AMELIA M. GLASER AND YULIYA ILCHUK

TRANSLATED FROM THE UKRAINIAN WRITTEN BY HALYNA KRUK

A Crash Course in Molotov Cocktails

These poems of witness may be wrought from a horrendous war, composed in times of turmoil and void of leisure, yet the Ukrainian poet Halyna Kruk's mastery is evident on every page, the keenly observed scenes and perplexing details visualizing the dire situation of her country but also its people's defiance: "war doesn't suit the rest of the world / like mutilation with an evening gown: / the look's too heavy / the language too sharp / the details too brutal." Kruk's poems grapple with the bare existential questions, every so often turning into prayer, into conversations with a merciless god, pleading to not "quiet the voice of anger." What do you take with you when "even keys / are non-essential"? How to maintain hope when realizing that human warmth may be deadly in times of war and its thermal imaging devices, how to cope with the loss of certainties while grasshoppers keep on chirping and shells are landing on the fields like birds of passage? Sometimes tender, offering surprising moments of stubbornly persisting beauty, sometimes bitter and hard, Kruk's poems are also a reminder for the rest of the world to "take us in, like unpleasant medicine." A necessary and powerful collection.

there and back again

i traveled there on tranquilizers,
back on painkillers
there were no other routes

i felt so shattered,
feared i'd pierce the aircraft cabin,
the hotel's interior was so intricately designed,
the interlocutors' bodies so beautiful

war doesn't suit the rest of the world
like mutilation with an evening gown:
the look's too heavy
the language too sharp
the details too brutal

let's close death's eyes with your hands, dear,
you can reach, you're closer there

we've got a special person for the hard conversations
we've got a special room
separate entrance and exit, not here, please

beautiful young bodies dive into the canal's waters,
sunlit, full of love, life, laughter
perfect, audacious, like
German pre-war postcards
a healthy spirit in a healthy body
carefully selected grains with no blemishes,
as we once were, sure of ourselves, love-filled

in the face of death i say to you:
love me as if there will never be
enough light to find each other again

love me until it seems
death's turned a blind eye,
but she's spying, from now on always everywhere
we know it, we can't finish

the war's taking care of our future,
as they say
as they see it

when you call from the war
birds are chirping
so the world still exists

i return on a bus full of quiet children

i return on a bus full of quiet children, silent mothers
with bundles of winter clothes from distant lands
where they were safe but unhappy,
sad, eyes looking back
where they waited each night for a return trip
longing to meet someone, anyone
to tell them their cities were still there
not made-up homes drawn by children
beneath a sun, because everyone knows the sun,
but home — far from everyone,
but dad or mom — not everyone.
it takes so long to relearn pre-war things, former skills,
even longer than coming home from various countries
longer than forgetting the sound of explosions, someone's dying
scream, the empty water canister shared by everyone
in that basement, who stayed in that basement.
a boy draws a cat without a leg,
and the people who never came out, and he draws himself, silent.
with a red felt pen, red screams for everyone
and black buries the ones who didn't come out

the bus carries us home through the night past memories on the roadside
past fear that neither home nor city is there

God, don't quiet the voice of anger

God, don't quiet the voice of anger
the voice of those who sit, forgotten, in shelters,
the voice of those who remain in the debris,
the voice of those who scream falling asleep,
the voice of those who can't close their eyes,
the voice of those who are speechless, mute, who stutter,
the voice of those who are dying of thirst and hunger,
the voice of those who gather bravery's crumbs,
the voice of those whose bodies stopped the columns,
who threw themselves between the bullets and the defenseless
the voice of the one howling, calling out in the emptiness,
the one who curses, who hides her face in grief
in her child's body, in her son's photo, in her mother's things,
in stooped shoulders, in trembling old knees
the voice of a burned out house, the voice of blood,
the voice of reason that's begun to doubt itself
the voice that drowns out sirens,
that rocks the yet unborn and the nameless
let it emerge from the throat choked with fear,
from the body that will turn to dust, from the city under fire,
from the heart that will beat for us all from now on, God, hear it,
the voice of hatred in a world where the voice of love can do so little

mangled blossom

mangled blossom
guilty of nothing
unswaddled in your eternity

from which tree will the wind blow
the fruits, if the fire burns the flowers down,
and the world goes out, a bud of hope

i tried to speak up
hard words, they come back to where they started
here was our garden. maybe not the garden of Eden,

but children babbled here,
birds fluttered to the branches and blue sky
i had yet to learn how much it hurts

that it could hurt a hundred times more

golden circle of perfection,
do you really care so little about flowers?
can nature replace
humankind with another creation?

however simple
and unique, everything longs to live

i throw the chaff to the wind
in hopes that at least the wind may sprout

gray zone

that was the summer they found a wasp nest,
and anybody with the nerve poked a stick at it and ran,
dad's old jacket, left hanging on a nail,
lay her heavy sleeve on his shoulder
comforting him as best she could.

that fall, when the neighbor's house caught fire from the sinking sun,
when no one but him ran to put it out, where had they gone?
he realized the collapsed event horizon
keeps the light from him, but it's there somewhere, where the seams come ap
it hits one spot over and over

that winter, when even in a mad dog's eyes
he ceased to look human, forgot to tell day from night, grew indifferent
to everything, warmed himself with another's blood, the price
of survival, nature devoured mound upon mound of people,
finding them, hiding them

that spring, when the war was over, they shot the wild animals,
cleared the debris, moved towns
to new empty places, and no one knew who this guy was
walking around in dad's jacket, talking to the plums that survived in the orch
and the plums answered.

in this house

in this house
the body of a poem, still warm,
hangs on the nail of the mundane
touched to its core
like a reproach, like proof,
that i was here
and you were here
and there was something between us
irresistible as breathing
uncertain as a kiss
unimportant to anyone but us

i love in you the possibility,
which we haven't used up,
the road, which we could have walked,
but didn't,
the choice, which we didn't make,
wanting it all at once
instead of a little bit
at a time

sometimes a poem turns into a house,
that you build at the edge of an abyss,
entirely out of a need
to overcome reality

PTSD

a stranger, like a bullet in the body
sits, smoking, doesn't look
doesn't ask when you'll be back
the road from home is under fire
the road home doesn't exist at all
he believed retreat was impossible
prepared this protective web
brought it straight to the heart
like a needle, but it was a pine-needle,
that smelled like home
the exit from this world seemed
even narrower than the entrance

he could have said: come here, woman
i won't let you go,
two are enough to start a world

he could have said, let's go, woman
we'll make it through together

he says, go away, woman, so long as there's silence
there's nothing living left in me
but you

be honest with yourself

be honest with yourself, honest as you can, like there's nothing left to lose:
we've leaned too long on others — so it's written, so folks say,
we're so used to embroidered straitjackets
to elaborate church feasts and rites
to flipping the bird behind our backs in defiance.

be straight with yourself: there won't be enough villages and towns left for
          us all to be peripheral
not enough soldiers to march single-file on the field
not enough fields, not enough Nankeen cloth imported from China.

be ruthless with yourself, no burying your head in the sand,
no reaching for your grandfather's glory and the memory of heroes
like you reach for a handkerchief to wipe patriotic tears and snot,
no disappearing into some sad song.

tell yourself:

i am я — last letter in the alphabet, without which there can be no me
i am the last land
i am what i can't give up
i am the carpenter of the beam in my own eye
i need not build a cross from it if i don't want
i can't give away what isn't mine
i belong to this people, i am this people
i don't want us to walk toward a dead end forever,
and so, i begin with me, break bounds

i am we. я ми *яму*: holes in the ground.

JORIE GRAHAM

To 2040

A question that by sparing its question mark assumes all the weight of an irrefutable and relentless answer ("Are we extinct yet.") lures us into Jorie Graham's *To 2040*, a moving and unsettling vision of an imminent future, of a present already on the brink of perdition, yet at the same time a declaration of love to a world that will cease to exist or, if it continues to be, then without us to laud it. In this most tender of apocalyptic poems, doing without the outworn images of doom and only hinting at a strange rising sun, at gold that "seems chipped from / what used to be Venice" (and, subdued, at the frailty of the body), Graham encourages us to listen, to look, to stand still, to marvel and deplore while we still can: "the stream. It is a temple. It is / rushing. How could we / not have heard." With lines of great brevity and mobility, leading up to and culminating in a coda of utmost sensuality, in the intense portrait of a long-awaited rain almost tangible on the reader's face, we are invited to ponder the bloom and the losses, the natural phenomena and their anything-but-commonness, encountering the light and "the distance in it—its howling—its gigantic / memory" as well as a raven whose "coat is / sun." A superb elegy, as thoughtful as it is thought-provoking, a virtuoso plea for curiosity and care, admonition and celebration at once.

Are We

extinct yet. Who owns
the map. May I
look. Where is my
claim. Is my history

verifiable. Have I
included the memory
of the animals. The animals'
memories. Are they

still here. Are we

alone. Look
the filaments
appear. Of memories. Whose? What was
land

like. Did it move
through us. Something says nonstop
are you here
are your ancestors

real do you have a
body do you have
yr self in
mind can you see yr

hands—have you broken it
the thread—try to feel the
pull of the other
end—says make sure

both ends are
alive when u pull to
try to re-enter
here. A raven

has arrived while I
am taking all this
down. In-
corporate me it

squawks. It hops
closer along the stone
wall. Do you remember
despair its coming

closer says. I look

at him. Do not
hurry I say but
he is tapping the stone
all over with his

beak. His coat is
sun. He looks
carefully at me bc
I am so still &

eager. He sees my

loneliness. Cicadas
begin. Is this a real
encounter I ask. Of the old
kind. When there were

ravens. No
says the light. You
are barely here. The
raven left a

long time ago. It
is traveling its thread its
skyroad forever now, it knows
the current through the

cicadas, which you cannot hear
but which
close over u now. But is it not
here I ask looking up

through my stanzas.
Did it not reach me
as it came in. Did
it not enter here

at stanza eight—& where

does it go now
when it goes away
again, when I tell you the raven is golden,
when I tell you it lifted &

went, & it went.

On the Last Day

I left the protection
of my plan & my
thinking. I let my self
go. Is this hope I

thought. Light fled.
We have a world
to lose I thought.
Summer fled. The

waters rose. How
do I organize
myself now. How do I
find sufficient

ignorance. How do I

not summarize
anything. Is this mystery,
this deceptively complex
lack of design. No sum

towards which to strive. No
general truth. None.
How do I go without
accuracy. How do I

go without industry.
No north or
south. What shall I
disrupt. How find

the narrowness. The
rare ineffable
narrowness. Far below
numbers. Through and behind

alphabets and their hiving, swarming—here,
these letters. I
lean forward
looking for the anecdote

which leads me closer to

the nothing. I do not

lack ideas. I do not
fail to see
how pieces
fall together. I do

not fail to be
a human companion
to the human. I am
not skeptical. I

am seeking to enter the in-
conspicuous. Where the stems
of the willows
bend when I

step. *There is dream in
them* I think. *There is
desire.* From this height
above the ground I see

too much. I need
to get down, need to
get out of the reach
of the horizon. Are

these tracks from this
summer or how many years
ago. Are these
grasses come again now,

new. This is being
remembered. Even as it
erases itself it does not
erase the thing

it was. And gave you.

No one can tell the whole story.

Translation Rain

I am writing this in code because I cannot speak or say
the thing. The thing which should be, or I so wish
could be
plumbed fathomed disinterred from this silence, this ever thickening
silence through which, once, the long thin stalks & stems, first
weaker weeds then branching &
stiffening, steadying &
suddenly sturdier—
strong enough to carry the seen—*the seeming* autocorrect reminds me—
the meaning my mind offers rushing in here
such that I must pull it back here—
grew. They, or is it *it*
grew. I
turn to the dead more now,
clearer every day as I approach them,
there in their silky layers of
silence, their wide almost waveless ocean,
rolling under their full moon,
swells striating the horizonless backdrop,
extending what seems like forever
in that direction—
though what can forever mean where there is
no space no time. I breathe
that in
and stare at it. I breathe,
I have an *in* and
out. I should have mentioned earlier this autocorrected to
breed. I had thought to ignore it but what a strange thing
how we expanded,
spread ourselves in smaller and smaller bits
across the natural world
until we were so thin with participation we
fell away.
Remember the code says the away.

But I was saying
how finally the rain will come. *Finally it will* I say in the code—&
you do intuit my meaning do you
not. It is a rain I have waited for all my life—
why do I see it only
now for what it
is—yes bronze as the sun tries to hang on—
then all these platinums braiding its freedoms,
coursing to find every crevice, loosen every
last stitch &
go in. It will touch everything. It will make more of the
more. More says my baffled soul, yes more.
It will push itself through & more deeply through till *all* must grow.
And yet we pray for it.
We thought it would never come.
Something *did* come says the code.
But *it* did not come.
Not in reality.
We thought it was an ideal.
Therefore it must come.
But it did not come.
How I wish I could say *free*. And yet we are not free it
seems. Or are we.
Each word I use I have used before.
Yet it is not used, is it? It is not used up, is it? Because what is in it stays
hidden. And the words
appear again as if
new. *Rain*, I say. *Rain now.*
And the black ocean shows itself in infinite detail because of the moon.
No matter that all is not lit.
Much remains because much remains hidden.
And you, are you there in the hidden—
nothing is rare,
all gleams.
And you there, gather these words up now & store them as seed.

Wait for the next rain.
In the world we lost there are those who knew if the lifesaving
rain would
come in time—if it would
actually fall—not pass us by again as a prediction, as
mist. They knew from
the birds. I
am still here with the birds for this while longer.
I do not know what they say.
Dust rises.
Evening sets.
I listen to the chatter.
I remember the clatter of sudden rain. The clapping of it onto the
hard soil.
The birds roost.
Among them a silence now & one singer briefly singing. Then silence.
We must all wait together.
There is no way to know.
It did not come.

They Ask Me

why the new
flawless birds
wired to perfection
whose beauty

song flight lift
hover settle you
cannot tell from
those not coming

back are not the
same, whose
feathertips shine
as if in the old

sunlight, whose
speckled wings
mottle further with
perfect shadow-speckle,

whose necks have
the sweet up/down
jerk of worry, whose
throat is made to

throb so slightly
as was the case
when song was
expelled why

do they not satisfy
us, why it is
only if we shut our
eyes the trills—

you can choose
the kind of bird—are
real, they come
to our sills, they leave

unexpectedly bc we
move…How they
flocked up across our
fields. How

that last morning,

in that world, in rising ground-

mist, in the pull of its fast
evaporation as that strange
sun rose, arms
outstretched &

laughing, out of
breath, we ran to chase them
till they dis-
appeared.

In Reality

the river was still widening as it went, as it carried me, thick mists rising
off it all day,
was still widening, yes, for a while longer, holding
the sky in its belly and back,
me on my back in the small of
my boat, rudder jammed, oar
lost or is it I tossed it
some long time ago
when I imagined myself
to be free. In the distance I see, reflected in the spooling,
a pair of spyglasses lifted
by the surveyor—fitted out for life—and it seems he is laughing
at what he sees, so magnified, light splaying over the surfaces,
the smeared faces of kings
whose lands are now vanquished,
clouds folding in the waters their rolled-up blankets
no longer needed for the ceremonies, the dancing,
controlling ebb, controlling
flow,
& like candy the benzenes the tankers before me have trailed,
& like wedding veils the foam made of monies,
a few millennia of monies,
no slack in that accrual,
no slowdown in that accumulation—we were fitted out
for life, armed with evolution & imitation,
trees casting their calligraphies deeper and deeper as they try to tell
the story of the bend we are now
approaching. A parrot flew over. It crossed the whole
river. I took a moment to sit up and
watch. Took in the setting. Took in the
dead forest, the ruined brick smokestack just visible
from a clearing, some columns still standing beyond it
someone's unyielding idea of
happiness.

Everything hangs in the balance, say the looping vines
the late red light begins articulating. Think about it, they scrawl,
try to remember
what it was you loved, try to clean up your memories
in time. The dragonflies begin as I lie back down.
I try to recall how I've gotten this far.
Every wing in the swarm also benzene-rainbowed
& clouding me
as we round the bend—& everywhere their eyes, their thousands of eyes.
They see nothing we see I think, and
am I a ghost now,
my left eye stung shut,
my right eye trying to make out what's up ahead
as the light goes gold.
Isn't it beautiful the old world says.
I try to remember. My one eye weeps.
Along the bank I make out the easels now. I see smocks and palettes,
and always that one hand up in the air
tapping & pointing, caressing the emptiness
through which whatever it is
they are seeking
arrives. Then down it goes
onto its canvas.
Represent me says the day. Quick. There's no time to lose.
Represent my million odors.
Represent my shaking grasses
the wind picks up and the river narrows and the dream of forgiveness is replaced
by desire.
Forgive me I think as the silt everywhere widens.
The light is failing. The dried banks show through.
Now the surveyor is packing his tools.
I feel his gaze cross my forehead inadvertently, feel the painter's gaze
brush my eyes without knowing.
The smoke from the dead stack is filling the river,
though it's just the riverbed coming up to meet us.

The lover of dead things flies by gingerly.
First bats swing across so absent of greed.
I look down at my hands, the air shrieking a little.
I figure the new swarms will be mosquitoes.
I lie in my going. I have nothing to contribute.
The world was always
ready for the world.
The river is running thin.
I see the fish on the banks with no birds around them.
Human heart, I say to myself, what are you doing here, this is far too much
for you to lay
eyes on.
The young fish float in the brackish water.
The slowing current. The cries of the dusk birds like shattering glass,
one cry and they're done.
To whom am I singing.
The winning ticket is still in my pocket.
The disappearing lovers are still in my satchel.
I have the stories we needed ready.
I understand the comings and goings called grief.
It is then that I see the river is ending.
The dusk hits its silver.
It thinks it's a jackpot.
The water is down to a handful of jewels
tossed out here and there on the miles of dry sand.
That's all I recall.
Then the keel hits and I'm tipped over gently,
as if to be fully & finally
poured out.
I am told by the cracks in the sand the whole length of the bed
to get up now, to *gather*
belongings. I am told to hurry & join the line,
to take my place, prepare my
ticket, & if I have a chance
to *choose*

disappearance. Told I might still get lucky,
might still get out.
Out to where, I wonder, looking back at my skiff,
at the millions of hulls
in this dried bend,
supplies strewn everywhere on the dead bed,
flashlights in dusklight picking us out.
Almost invisible, the plastics gleam…
Thus it was we came to no longer reach the ocean.
Flow rate failed. Flow direction failed. Surface water dis-
appeared. Subsurface
dried. I remember the spring, the headwaters, precipitation, swell.
I see again the currents
begin—the sweet cut into land of
channels, meanders. Remember the
turns. Put my hands
in the springs,
the groundwater recharge. The slow delicate fanning
of the drainage basin. The mouth, the confluence,
the downriver arrivals—
delta—sediment yield—salt tide—
open sea.

Can You

hear yourself
breathe. Can you help
me. Can you
hear the fly. Can you

hear the tree. No
I don't mean wind,
I mean the breathing of
the tree through

bark. Can u, say the grasses,
please hear
us. Can we hear u hear
the tips of water on

us, lithe &
so heavy with light & bending
lens-tips. Can u
hear this e-

vaporation. Can u
keep
blessing, keep not
thinking, remind

yourself of

your own

breathing, & what
is growing—leaves root sap, sun
forcing the flower....
Moving this way

you'll see you can hear
soil breathe,
& in it, working to get thru it,
the worm,

& each turning of it
by the worm, hear, &
the breathing in it
of the worm, hear. Moving this way

you'll hear the earth go on
without you—
when u are
no longer

here, when u are

not breathing. The fish the
water the sand the
needle in the pine. The here. Hear it
breathing

as it turns,
and as now in it turns
the effort
of this worm.

This Vase of Quince Branches You Sent Me

in blossom. On the
kitchen table now.
Taller than me.
Why do I feel

ashamed.
In my warm vest and winter coat.
In tears.
Hands empty at my

side. What are you
for. Standing there as if in
some other country. An
otherwise. Without

past or future.
No logic religion sorrow
thought. Whispering
smoke signals to

morninglight.
Are you hearing each other. The sight of me
is of a thing with
too much heart,

too much—

salmon-pink blossoms brutal with
refusal of
meaning—why
am I

ashamed. Dear
tree,
I have watched
where u welled up and broke skin to

emerge like a disaster
of beauty, yr
tall arms here reach up &
out

differently, cut branches carefully criss-
crossed in the vase to arrange u, to hold u
firm in the
design. And the water

which you draw in at
each white
cut. I struggle
to stand at

appropriate
attention. Yr sweet acrid scent
reaches me
now. Something else

floats in the air
around yr blossoms.
It stares at me.
It keeps on staring. If it's

screaming
I can't tell. It's not domesticated.
The rest of yr tree arrives like a bloodshot eye
in my head. Silence is

stretching. There is less and less
time. I breathe
quietly. I place my hands on my
eyes. If I am a messenger, what is

my message. I fear
it is fruitless. It is un-
yielding. It is devoid of
patience. I reach

out. My fingers try for
no damage. But my mind is still here.
It envelops everything.
I think of the invisible stars. I try to

unthink them. I would give that
unthought space back
to yr branches.
Some of yr buds are

darker & swollen.
They have not opened yet.
What is it to open.
What is it to open & have one's

last time left.
The green is coming. It is pushing from behind.
I can feel the tremor of hanging on.
I have not yet fallen.

How crowded we are on our stalk.

Then the Rain

after years of virga, after
much *almost*
& much *never again*, after
coalescing in dry

lightning & downdrafts & fire,
after taking an alternate
path thru
history & bypassing

us, after the trees,
after the gardens,
after the hard seeds
pushed in as deep as

possible & kept alive on dew,
after the ruts
which it had once cut
filled in with

dust & molds—& pods
that cannot sprout—
not even the birds
came—& old roads

began to reappear—

after the animals,
after the smallest creatures
in their tunnels & under
their rocks,

after it all went, then,
one day,

out of in-
terference & dis-

continuity, out of in-
congruity,
out of collision
somewhere high above our

burnt lands, out of
chemistry, unknowable
no matter how
quantifiable,

out of the touching of one atom by an
other, out of the
accident of
touch, the rain

came.

We thought it was
more wind. Something tapped
the peeling roof.
We knew it was not

heat ticking, our secret imaginary
birds. We knew it by the smell which filled
the air re-
minding us, what did it

remind us of, that smell,

as if the air turned green,
as if the air were the deep in-
side of the earth

we can never reach
where *it* reaches out to
those constellations we have not
discovered, not named, & now
never will,

and which are not dead, no—

And it brought memory. But of
what. So long. Where are you my
tenses. The crowns
rattled again, harder, & again we thought

wind. I pressed
the rusted screen-door
& stepped out. Was I afraid? Where it hit
dust whirled up

in miles of refusals—stringy, flaring,
as if flames could be dust,
faster with each landing, till it
tamed them & they

lay down again as earth,
and were still,
and took it in
everywhere,

& when I sat on the low wall
it slid over my features,
& my neck held runnels,
as if I were a small book

being carefully perused for
faults, ridges, lapses of

time in my thought—
because I could not recall it—
my skin could not,

my hands could not,

I look at them now

with my eyes full of rain,
and they say hold us up,
you are not dying
yet, we are

alive in the death
of this iteration of
earth, there will be another
in which no creatures like us

walk on this
plateau of years & minutes & grasses &
roads, a place where
no memory can form, no memory of

anything, not again, but for now
the windowpanes shake as the
harder rain hits
and the stiff grasses bend over &

the thing which had been a meadow once
releases a steam,
& if you listen you can hear
a faint pulse in it,

a mirage, a release of seeds into the air

where wind insists, & my heavy
hands which rise now, palms up, shining,
say to me,
touch, touch it all,
start with your face,

put your face in us.

ISHION HUTCHINSON

School of Instructions

Primordial elementals are here: we are by the sea, in the desert, in the trenches, in the mind of a schoolchild discovering "natural" history, in vibrant daily life, in anabasis of war, and studying the innocent volunteers going to disease and slaughter. *School of Instructions* is a transcendent, hybridic feast of a book, an innovative, condensed epic comprising startling poetry, primary sources, Biblical naming and mapping, and a haunting trajectory of the British Empire's Middle Eastern campaigns of WWI juxtaposed with twentieth-century Jamaica. Hutchinson's brilliant transmission is deeply intuitive and profound as scholarly and poetic gnosis—you feel instructed by the ongoing koan, coil, knot of colonialism ingrained with civilization.

Selections from "His Idylls at Happy Grove"

Agog with corrosive dates in his book,
Godspeed shuttled between bush and school,
branching with delirium. He recalled
rain gauzed cannons with steam. Escutcheons
fluttered a red-letter day of sorrow:

> *Every man who went from Jamaica to
> the front was a volunteer. 10,000.*

Volunteer? *Bourrage de crâne.* Shadowed chains.
Sails, the air stagnate, white flashes of sharks
haunting fevers strangers shared in the hulls,
never to break after centuries on land;
perpetual flashes, perpetual sharks

trailing men who sang on the *Verdala*
in a blizzard to war.
                            Recover them.

They shovelled the long trenches day and night.

Frostbitten mud. Shellshock mud. Dungheap mud. Imperial mud.
Venereal mud. Malaria mud. Hun bait mud. Mating mud.
1655 mud: white flashes of sharks. Golgotha mud. Chilblain mud.
Caliban mud. Cannibal mud. Ha ha ha mud. Amnesia mud.
Drapetomania mud. Lice mud. Pyrexia mud. Exposure mud.
    Aphasia mud.
No-man's-land's-Everyman's mud. And the smoking flax mud.
Dysentery mud. Septic sore mud. Hogpen mud. Nephritis mud.
Constipated mud. Faith mud. Sandfly fever mud. Rat mud.
Sheol mud. Ir-ha-cheres mud. Ague mud. Asquith mud. Parade
    mud.
Scabies mud. Mumps mud. Memra mud. Pneumonia mud.
Mene mene tekel upharsin mud. Civil war mud.
And darkness and worms will be their dwelling place mud.
Yaws mud. Gog mud. Magog mud. God mud.
Canaan the unseen, as promised, saw mud.

They resurrected new counterkingdoms,
by the arbitrament of the sword mud.

Selections from "The Anabasis of Godspeed"

XXVIII

The moon was high up in RAMLEH. The surrounding
camps were bombed and machine gunned by enemy
aircraft that visited nightly. Bel the old back-of-bush
shanty shiftshaper blasting thunderbolts in RAMLEH.
Coolie royal Rosalie retraced herself to untouchable. The
southeastern sky was a single collapsing star. Rin tin tin
tin. He hid in latrine stalls from rickets-brained
Sadducees on patrol. Nocturnal birds cried out but only
one died because they were hidden in the moon
darkened olive grove of RAMLEH.

Then again at Christmas the boy's hands were high with
the murder of sorrel. He was told to whitewash the
long walls of Exodus Funeral Supplies & Services in
ANNOTTO BAY. Heat spangled the seaside as he
muttered in acute Estrangela: "Amen I was seized. Amen
again I was not seized. Amen I suffered. Amen again I
did not suffer."

XXX

In the Quaker chapel alone Godspeed stared at the white
 angels and the luxe-hair Christ painted above the
 baptismal pool. He thought of the nub of magnet like a
 single black eye still whirling on the stalled fan. Then
 proceeded through the reeds and hawks of UPPER
 EGYPT to the tamarisks and hornets of LOWER EGYPT
 and from there to JERUSALEM where No. 9265 Pte. J.
 Floras "A" boy died from dysentery. *Ha-ha-ha-hassatan* he
 sneezed and left the chapel. The stars went out and the
 torches in the dark trembled like the curtains of
 MIDIAN trembling to the wind.

Electric flares off the tips of horses' ears running forwards
 with teeth clenched against the burning khamsin. The
 battalion drifted in the distance and some of the very
 foolish men swore they saw Hannibal crossing the ALPS.
 Trah-la-la-la.

XXXI

Jamaica Broadcasting Corporation meteorologist Roy
Forrester promised rain. Once again no rain came. But a
hurricane the prime minister said was like HIROSHIMA
because it blew away all the island's fowls to FLORIDA
only to return as high tariff frozen chicken backs and
necks which Godspeed scorned and never ate. Then
proceeded with rapid succession to SHARTA and DEIR
SENEID 7 miles N. OF GAZA. Whilst there they saw
corpses and corpses of the dead from the 52nd Division
lying about. The men were repulsed by a charnel stench
they could not staunch. These were buried. Not in peace.

The battalion was equipped and issued box respirators PH
gas helmet being withdrawn and returned to ordnance.
The boy was issued a blue shell inhaler by visiting
Canadian nurses. He shook it and heard the babble of
End Times. A puff. Cloudburst in his shipwrecked chest.
He coughed and swore to bring about the Parousia.

The strength of the battalion stood at 24 officers and 915
other ranks.

LXIV

Then into MOUNT EPHRAIM and SHARON then on to
  JERICHO and AMMAN then through SAMARIA to
  GILEAD and GALILEE then on to DAMASCUS and
  finally through the gross darkness of CANAAN to
  SHILOH the battalion glimmered its nocturnal corolla
  of petals towards its last School of Instructions fragrant
  of memories chastened of sacrifice sweetened of
  resignation quickened of hope in the front line for
  untold harm to carry ammunition to do the general
  work or something like that to simply be men merciful
  men whose righteousness must not be forgotten.

After Godspeed lost the precept of his head he lost his mind
  and found it in the larvae of bees outside EIN GEDI
  where he exalted himself like a young palm tree. He wept
  again this time into song for he knew where there was
  anger there will be grief.

Selection from "Three Heroic Emblems"

Where the sun never conceded to light,
now lit. Even still, belated justice
does not reflect where it must show: England:
leave room for the beloved below;
recover them all, for belated praise.
A whiff of incriminating cherries
holds beneath the meridian blue,
raises choppy flatlines of the Atlantic
into vertical columns, heavenwards,
which is the earth. Earth which is their bodies
that have crossed, above deck, the sea-earth,
and give the earth a lasting heritage,
and the sea the broad church of night and day.

In Praise of a Shadow

Source of echo
madman of prophecies
buffering nonsense
in absence of anything
solid as cloud
flung
from the womb
pale pallid asteroid
belt of nanny goat

conjuror of the ill-spoken
adlibbing in shadow
a race in a curve
as an old woman's palm
billows the blue light
instance of an ant's
legs twitch beneath
the headless Nobody
trickster and soothsayer

burner of Ark
cutter of dub
double-talk lame-walker
translating ship screams
and the long gazes
and the neck cricks
and the hollow face
celestial and earthbound
posing the first question
to God after an eagle
picked your liver
and tell the reply
in the treetops
to hold still

and accept
fade and descent
into nothing
like a scribbler train
heading into a bright
blind and flat
as the mouth hole
of some strange being
and what you say
at the controls
picking up signals
and feedback
off the metallic horizon
and the purple field

where a girl
undoes her hair
and warps herself
around a tree
her mother is buried
under the grass
there you once wept
from whence comes
something longer
than a shadow
when a shadow
falls in the desert

and the hills expire
the sea expires too
for you outlived
your mule days
of packed crocus
and blades of sun

ripe on your back
at the river
like a crab catcher
in shortcuts
rancid with obeah
on your skin
for a few shillings
to blast off downtown

praise your tongue
praise your spirit
praise your madness

in praise of fern
in praise of shame-me-lady
in praise of bushel
in praise of hanging leaves
in praise of praising

your word mass
your mix match
your jamming of elements

when things get terrible
and times get dread
you're ahead

praise
praise
praise

ANN LAUTERBACH

Door

Ann Lauterbach has brought together a suite of remarkable poems in her dazzling book *Door*, which troubles and stirs the paradox: the place for "self" in mediated space. Her door is the existential hinge of the poetry. A poem is a door. A book is a door. We construct doors to keep probing eyes away. We shut ourselves into scriptoriums to convene with fear and hope, struggling how to weave the poem, what do we allow. Lauterbach's tableaus, her subtle, multivalent sound and panoramic consciousness—all shimmering, generous. She magnetizes others to enter and deeply inhabit the sweep of her uniquely crafted, exquisite poetry.

Habitat

Do not partition or curtail the fearful crowd.
They are already stranded.
Your belts and sandals will not reach them
in their wandering distress. I myself will be
wearing a stole, with tassels.
Sometimes choices are words; sometimes they
come as tactile objects to be touched.
The contingent of insurgent migrants
moving swiftly over the stark terrain, they
have no time for these niceties, or what is
kept under our vestments, dangerously
excitable. Today in the shower I was recalling
orgasm as a layered volume of flow
so intricately woven as to be the sensed motion
of time slowly opening. Now at last it is raining.
These weathers are included as reminder
that our inner and outer
beings are breathing into the seams of the day
and that the temporal scansion
is as uninhabitable as a rainbow.
The clock, however, is full of accusations
and praise meted out
into the days; it cannot know

the barefoot figures

fleeing toward the harbor, their faces

illumined, their limbs arcing into shadow wings.

It cannot know how light dilates evening.

And dreams, what of them? Will they bleed

through, find a way to tell of our passage,

relate grass and stream,

three coyotes basking on the hill,

swirl of cloud, the hawk's high whistle,

no camera, no lamp, no held image

to capture the unpredictable path?

Enlightenments, vistas,

storied performances; everyone up close

and sweaty with desire; montage

of the nameless boy

with his entourage of lovers.

They climbed to the top of the spire

as I watched, the boy and two girls,

wearing blue shorts that flared in the wind,

and then they could not find a way down,

their bodies entangled in metal casements.

Meanwhile, branches had been collected

and arranged, stapled to a wall,

but no one had thought to find water

so they began to wither, their leaves

browned and stiff, and the woman

from the gallery wept, and tore her skirt

into ribbons that the bowerbirds took.

The bowerbirds weren't in the dream. They

are a distraction; you can look them up on

TikTok, where there are other

pranks, jokes, dances

and tricks that resemble dreams.

What happened? The secular spirit

gropes for solace and refuge.

The painter could see the scene,

depicting the sainted monk

in his habit among birds;

depicting the ravished angels

strewn across the blue wall's

firmament in a storm of grief.

These figments,

stories without witness,

rendered as material fact.

And so we stare at their silence,

its reservoir of the miraculous offered on trust.

Garden

See! See! Comest thou now

quietly while the days are short

and our sleep pestered by gloom.

Come! Count sticks! Bright nature!

Sight after dark. The spot

where desire sleeps

as a gift and ceases its ancient

poison. But the serpent landed

elsewhere, blown by wind.

By then, it had no tongue

and so no way to speak.

Ribbons and wires

and silk threads were then woven—

Eve is hungry. Please conduct her

to the scene of nourishment,

sweet leaves and an apple dipped in dew.

Door

The Said closes, is closing, has closed the door.
John said, *I am the Door.* Who closed it?

And who will open it, if it is not shut
forever? This is the other question, called

from the balcony by the young Marine
in uniform, before the matches flame

and the entire arena is lit and flickering
with its own memory. Who is there?

These lights, knocks, hands,
faces, crowds, surges. *Who*

is there? The street flares again
in the mind's geography,

cascading out from the numerical
so everyone is passing, countless.

Anonymity caresses its dream

and you were there, inside me,

where no story can be told, but for

the passivity of the mute child.

2.

Is Door a wound?
Farther still, the hall is dark,

and a stranger is passing
across the threshold, entering under

rugs or blankets pulled across the small rusty
cot. She stood in the pond, her body drenched,

and the girl asked, *Don't you wash your face
before bed?* They were naked on the grass

when the iris bloomed, and the mother turned
away. There were others, another time,

perhaps by the sea, perhaps on the stairs,
where the scent of balsam and lavender pulsed.

Why be concerned? As if invited to share
a secret. The one behind the door?

There is nothing behind the door; there is only
door, a condition, a prospect, a

perception in which a gap occurs, or might

occur, and you can step into or across, you

can leap or fall, you can turn away, go back.

It's an open-and-shut choice; it's a dare.

3.

The story is always a dare. What sorrow
we have made. Earth wounded, ready to quit.

Where is the circle loved as we
went around on the great horses, riding up

down, down up, preparing? All the lit
matches; all the weak lights flickering

in the auditorium, the blasted church,
the Tree of trees. We sang along:

Yes, and how many times can a man turn his head
And pretend that he just doesn't see?

There's no one in this clearing. And the deer?
Gone from the hill, onto yesterday's

horizon. Some final animation presses down
as at the end of a film, and everyone

weeps for the lost child, for the dead doe.
The flames are lavender and gold,

licking at the charred edge of a log

as if there were no urgency.

When can I use my gun? When can I shoot?

A brute noise unsettles the open field.

4.

A drone tumbling across the sky
flagging its intent, and the unfolding

wings of a telescope. *Flap, flap*, hoarding space
only to crash into a holiday postponed

for eternity. Good we have *eternal*
so the gigabyte and its multiplication

can endure, the motherboard
go dim without consequence. I

will name my start-up
Terminal Eternal.

She got up from the bunk, damp,
and walked across the field

as the sun broke over a high ridge
and its splinters radiated outward

like transparent blades
and the air alive with atoms

of her previously intact reception,

her limbs and hair, her open mouth,

now only luminous breath,

immanent and atavistic as a spell.

5.

So those remaining
will forage for their facts

under the wood ash and the bones
of the putrid carcass decaying

in the underbrush.
The observed world will rescind

its rights to observation,
transitioned into the aperture

of an uncanny, sightless eye
careering through space

with its lidded wings
and enormous, engorged desire.

Where do we go? We dissolve,
ashes to dust, dust to an infinite

atmosphere turning its particulates
into noise, contamination, grace.

And there, there are no numbers

to calculate infinity; there is only infinity.

6.

Please do not address me as Team.
I am not a Team; I have not joined a Team.

Please do not address me as Friend.
I am not your Friend. I have never met you.

Please find another way of
counting on me other than by asking

for money. I don't understand
money. It frightens me.

Power frightens me.
I am not much good to you,

dear faceless, voiceless,
bodiless thing of the ask, dear

solicitous encounter with no one.
One hundred and six ships

backed up in the harbor and no market
for the mediocre; only

the latest, greatest will do.

I'm still waiting for

Christmas ornaments. Five cards

command, *Scratch & Win*.

7.

Forgotten discursive threshold.
Queasy opacity above, slick below,

fool's gold of the chronic impasse
between what is and what is not.

Marauding ravenous jays
wearing the uniform of the sky

plummet downward onto stones.
My father is a blue jay, dead on an attic floor.

There was no early warning, no sea breeze.
Now the future condemns

all our heralds to chiding,
indignant as crows. And the wind

thrashes at our stare, and something
leaks into the pond, some rust

found on the metal cage, the saw's ragged
edge. In winter, all our tools are silent.

8.

I know, such reading perpetuates
a stranded, stale vocabulary,

before the listing algorism
tested our mutability in exchange

for knowing the instrumental tally
of our accumulated dread,

our daily dead. The face changes. The heart
stumbles onto a clearing, as in

a painting whose surface
is a pattern rendered

as brilliant debris echoing across
the landscape, carrying our beliefs.

The layers are like a translucent cloth
flowing outward, sailing almost,

into the deep folds of a sunset,
its bloods spreading their wonder.

And this is thought, also, one

under another, waiting, colliding,

carrying all the partial images

as on a breath; phantom, unless said.

9.

Mirage, smoke and mirrors, lies.
What ails? What makes us want to stay

asleep forever, rather than awaken
to morning's fortune, as the door closes

on our skit of promise, our storied
enchantment, when we marched,

hands outstretched, singing,
onto the field, and the words spilled

into air like so many vagrant seeds
carried across, and down, and into

the river's bright agenda. Now flow coils
into an obsidian hole, and an old rake

hangs on the side of the fence
as if to entice us back into an alignment,

as if to alleviate the scheme's
reckless anomaly, its mute consent,

passed from one to another

like a masked kiss between lovers.

10.

Tenuous, the wire or thread or single line
drawn across, edge to edge,

or down to the wedge between
frame and floor, like a slip of moonlight,

an apparition where the footsteps
blur across and whatever is visible

retreats into the animate whisper
of fear. *Who is there?*

Turning away, or toward,
not answering the door, not ever

knowing who went out, came back,
went out, came back, went,

never came back. Tenuous, the sign
with the name, the false resemblance.

Waiting is a form of thought. Thought
turns away, unable to name its ancestry.

II.

Begin this imagining, pull together
whatever is unspoken, trace, enigma,

ghost plurality: the near and the other,
the mongrel dog and the brute brokers

of unspeakable acts. Is speech action?
Still the question haunting time,

just when——
Please conduct me to a place

where there are no calibrations and no outcomes.
I can hear the wind. It sounds the way

I imagine an aura might sound, hovering just
below sense, like an underpainting

never to be discovered but which is alive
with crimson, a wound, or a mouth; a smile

on the face of a stranger. The wind is louder now
but it has no word and so no origin.

How to name a sound? Call it Door.

I know what comes next; I remember this tune.

Alarm

The girl is an alarm. Her lust is always articulate.

—Lisa Robertson

Come here little girl

little green-eyed

        greedy girl

      come along the sacred dial   its fortune

              wheeling across a childless night   come

out from the damaged sphere of gods   do not look   they

are contained in marble   they are

not familiar with your pain   have no room

for choice

               as if to stagger the vocabulary   love into increments

as if to not dip down into the vulgate of dreams   *he he he*

touched *he* left   *he he*   smiled along the coastal lace

the bloodied sheets   ships ship   all the muscular boys all cause

shackled from that entourage to this   greedy girl   drowned

in the ancestral atmosphere   pulleys   landings   rocks   preachers   goods

          bloodied lace roiling along the coast the plantation shed

find the goodness find the burning brand fire seared   and sing

into the wasted lingo of hope o   greedy girl.

Chimes aggregate repetitive   coal sand pebble cloud crop

and the sad petals   white rose   brown on the floor   white rose

furiously   pure down to earth   greedy girl   comes down into earth

brown petals   this indictment   crime   the plural indictment

the force of a name   greedy girl   with your silver shoes your torn slip.

 Sniff the broken lobe, the soiled petals. Walk swiftly across the parched fie

Stay in the refrain of never no more

   walk swiftly   carry your dull weapons greedy girl your rusty blad

     your parcel of seed. Recall

  the stairwell and the toppled house   recall Jonah

   the flight out of Egypt   recall the rivers of Babylon

   recall smoke and the blistering flesh

   the scent of fear   greedy girl the towering flames

    rising over the circumference the blue peninsula

some psalm   some song   some dance   this way   some path

   come along

 greedy girl across the burning meadow approaching the roofs rising abov

  the stony earth

   plural rage   greedy girl   plural tears.

Door

And then we fell into the hands

of a person who had lost her keys, so

we were stranded

at the airport without a note, or an address,

free, ready to run

into halls dense with slogans and slots,

and the cold blue light of a fabricated dawn.

This image must be fictive, none of us is

traveling with another,

we are each on our own,

wearing the spotted pants of a clown

and listening to our own music, note

by note, not humming along

for fear of disturbing you, sitting on

that soiled bench in front of a door.

What is this story? Legend has it

she traveled alone so that she could see

everything more clearly. What she saw

she turned into something to say, and

what she heard she turned into

a different music, unaccompanied

by the crowd now racing into the screen.

On Relation

After a while, you run out of news and so words decline.
The better way would be not to worry about your news

or even the news. Words don't care about your or the
news. Words are indifferent to how you are feeling about

your feelings; they do not care if you see something or
say something. Words congregate among themselves

and are safe from your gestures, your desire
to have them meet you exactly where or as meaning

is. If you would look around, you would see
that words do not wish or care to be included

in your pursuit of the right, the perfect, the one.
They need not attach themselves to that this or this that.

Nocturne

It turns out there wasn't a door, so she stood looking at the wall, and then at the ground, and then again at the wall, and then up at the sky. The sky was doorless, which was comforting, especially at night, when she could make images from the stars by drawing lines between and among them, as the earliest persons had done as they walked along on the desert sand. But now, looking up into the brightly strewn array, she could not draw a door because the shapes she saw resembled other geometries and, although everything seemed infinitely open, there was no way through. Perhaps, she thought, I can draw something else, not a door, but simply a path; why would anyone want to be inside when the way through cannot be enclosed. Why am I sad that there is no door? she asked herself, and then she saw how she had turned in the night air, and found herself entirely enclosed. And she asked herself, How is it possible to be at once enclosed and illuminated.

Door

Small incident last among closings
a singular display confirmed

not the risky allowance of fate not
accruing slowly as in a habit

certainly not mere weather not
choosing a hinge or a lock

entity spreading outward voracious as oil
the collapsed wings trapped

a condition and its picture
what was once shuttered

allowing light in   allowing the moment
to resist passage yes

that endowment   the image
simple recursive

darkly enfolded—
ancient as night   traversing loss

and the abrasion

an appeal   to be   restored.

GEORGE MCWHIRTER

TRANSLATED FROM THE SPANISH WRITTEN BY HOMERO ARIDJIS

Self-Portrait in the Zone of Silence

Self-Portrait in the Zone of Silence brings poet-translator George McWhirter's adept English to the service of a great world-poet, Homero Aridjis. The book's enchanting variety of tones and subjects expresses a rounded human being engaged with our total experience, from the familial to the political, from bodily sensations to dream, vision, philosophic thought, and history, from hope to foreboding. A keynote is the sense of a person speaking with us plainly and yet from kinship with a light that bathes, and springs from, each thing.

Meeting with My Father in the Orchard

Past noon. Past the cinema
with the tall sorrowful walls
on the point of coming down, I enter the orchard.
Show over, all of them have gone:
day laborers, dogs, and doors.
My father is standing in front of a fig tree.
My mother has died, the children, grown old.
He's alone, small threads of air
weave in and out of his tattered clothes.
For fear of getting too close and startling him
with my living presence, I want to go straight by,
the stranger now with white hair whom he asks,
"Who's that there?"
"Father it's me, your son."
"Does your mother know you're back? Will you stay and eat?"
"Father, for years now your wife has lain at rest
by your side in the town graveyard."
Then, as if he has divined everything,
he calls me by my childhood name
and gives me a fig.
So we met up, the living and the dead.
Then, each went on his way.

The Sacrificial Stone

In a voice so loud the slave singing appeared about to burst open his chest.
—Fray Bernardino de Sahagún,
General History of the Things of New Spain

All those rituals at the break of day, what for?
All those branch-bedecked altars, to honor who? All those conches
    and flutes sounding—on account of what?
And that priest with the paint-spattered face, what's he here for?
Those dancing all around me, I don't know them.
That one, laid out there on the sacrificial stone, is not me.
My homeland lies on the far side of that hill.
My god is a different god.
My head spins to the beating boom-boom on the drums
and the rays of sunlight that beam back off the walls.
With hair shaved off the crown of my head
and legs painted with red and white stripes,
drunk on blue pulque, inebriated with terror,
soon I shall forfeit my heart
soon I will be the god who slaughters me.

The Sun of the Blind

That evening six-o'clock sun
setting like a sob
between the buildings.

That vagabond sun
that is taking a seat
on the vacant barbers' chairs.

Sun that strums
the strings of a guitar
with trembling hands like a lover.

That sun passing over your hair
and crashing onto the black
shades of the blind busker.

The sun on Gante Street
that lights up the dark face
of the little girl in the window.

Sun of those black eyes
looking at how the old hands
pluck out strains of blood and shadow.

Sun of the blind.

Garden of Ghosts

1

The pear tree with its pears isn't aware it's a ghost.
Geraniums, roses, bougainvillea,
trailing over the ground in a lapsed splendor
of purple petals, are unaware of their own absence.

All are gone. The women visiting,
the rains, the goldfinches, dogs,
the creaking of doors, the voices, gone,
and you alone, my invisible mother, are here.

2

Birds drawn on the blue notebook of the mountain,
childhood angels drowned in a basin
among the dried-up flowers of memory,
age-old mythologies scaling the walls
down which redknee spiders crawl,
transparent bodies in the passageways that come upon us
like a wind to lead the way to buried treasures,
nameless creatures that spy on us through cracks
in rickety doors that only the air moves,
pale figures, attempting to take shape on the mountain
when the sun has gone in are aspects of me,
quivering with unreality on the hill of gold.

3

Along the cobbled street
ran the little girl, Josefina,
dressed in percale and shadow

a bandit had come into town
by way of the graveyard to steal women
and was reaching arms out
to lift her up-and-onto his black horse

through the street she ran, terrified,
the small shadow with big eyes
who would one day be my mother.

4

I was not aware that flowers may be the ghosts
of their own morning and spook a boy who searches
for his reflection in the misted-over mirror of his empty room.

I wasn't aware that the flicker cast ahead of his steps
is like the whip of shadows left behind by an unremembered
relative on the floor tiles.

And that my deaf aunt with the white braids, so like
La Llorona,* who bathed me under the setting sun,
went about rapping on doors in the air.

Come, digger of graves from my childhood,
come and play in my garden of ghosts,
the game of love and death.

* La Llorona is a wailing ghost roaming the earth in search of her children,
whom she drowned.

Poet Beatific

I think of you, Land of Weir,
my house of water on the hill
my dreams in a naked crowd
      —Philip Lamantia, *Ekstasis*

He showed up one night at a café on the Alameda,
the trees were leafless, the President of the Republic
had just passed on his way to Los Pinos
leading a motorcade of bulletproof cars
and motorcyclists in sunglasses.

The poet beatific turned with surprise to see
those solemn vampires straight out of the Templo Mayor
for human sacrifices in Mexico-Tenochtitlan,
well, those Draculas certainly were plotting
to rob the poets of their word and their *ekstasis*.

With his lunar pallor—not out of any sickness,
but from the late-night vigils verse demands,
and the effect of the drugs, smoked, ingested
and anointed—the poet brought on his trances
on the pyramid of the sun and the solar mountain.

He saw no eternities in a grain of sand
like Blake, nor conversed with angels
in the streets of London, like Swedenborg,
he sought enlightenment off a cracked plate
and in the penumbras of a room on Oslo Street.

One night in the company of youngsters who came from up North
on a quest for the beatific, he scaled the Televicentro Tower,
which turned men into mindless swine,
and from up there pissed a rain of anger on its star performers
and the security police, who peered up at him from the sidewalk.

In the little church of Santa Maria, in a blue dress
and string of fake pearls, a woman (who spoke
the language of Rimbaud, but not his poetry)
married the poet beatific. Their honeymoon trip was a walk
in a corn field, under a black umbrella to ward off the sun.

Two individuals from the Drug Squad stole
his *ekstasis* one noontime when they detained him outside
the Wells Fargo office, confiscated the corpus delicti,
a couple of poems, and locked him up in the jail for foreigners
with thugs and guerrilla fighters from Cuba.

Photographed front and side he was deported.
The bribable judges, though not bribed by him,
asked him in the immigration prison, "Surname
and first name?" "Philip Lamantia." "Place of origin?"
"San Francisco." "Occupation?" "Poet beatific."

The Creation of the World by the Animals

(according to the Popol Vuh)

Across an empty darkness,
across unmoving sky,
flashed scarlet macaw—
so day broke; and yellow orioles
with turquoise eyes
began dancing a solo of light

and within a mighty ceiba tree,
the "mother of birds," appeared
a skinny spider monkey
his privates dangling—and howler monkey,
scriving prophesies on the mirror of dawn,
and a lunar owl, perched on death's arm.

Caiman lurked on a river bank,
his back marked with celestial stripes,
and sharp-fanged jaguar
pursued the fleeing deer; and eagle,
aloft on clear wings, spied the horizon—
and all was a feathered dream: yellow and green.

Then figured from water, clay, and wood,
came woman and man:
offspring of the sun,
children of forest and mountain,
with their eyes they could behold themselves,
their voices named the animals.

Heart of the Sky, Heart of the Sea
Heart of the Earth beat as one,
and all the winged creatures, creatures
of the waters and the land
could be, breathe, love, and cast shade.
And life is re-created every day.

Self-Portrait in the Zone of Silence

On the wall of the room there was a mirror
reflecting back a comical skull that was laughing at itself.
Jawbones knit together by the threads of death.

Behind that skull there was yet another and another.
Nothing broke the impact of the voiceless laugh suspended in the night
except one ray of moonlight.

I, in the after dream, was exceedingly pale, despite being painted
with the red pigment related to blood and fire
and with the insignia of Tezcatlipoca, god of the smoking mirror.

Noonday, there close-by and here-afar, began to boil,
and between the powerful jaws and claws of the yellow cat
the bones of a small doe were being crushed.

A black mirror reflected my solitary person.
A murky green enfolded the god of duality's silhouette,
half his face, fleshless, and an eye through which an empty train was
    passing.

The house among the dunes had a door that opened onto the infinite.
On a nopal, hearts were drying like the prickly pears on the cactus
beneath a searing sun that never set.

Facing starwards a windowpane was opening and closing.
In the dusk monkey scribes were dancing
and devouring black flowers and little smiling faces.

Chased by his own shadow, my dog Rufus was running under the
    moon.
Between dunes and evanescent rivers he searched for his
    resurrection.
Since the day of his death nobody had caught sight of him.

I was forty when this took place in the desert.
The winds of the soul told no hour and at the speed of forgetting
they ran through the darkness at one hundred kilometers per hour.

My lips burned and like tequila desire provoked violence
and lust in me for no reason. So, face to face with myself
I traced my way through labyrinths, anxieties, wrinkles, eyes and ears,

jawbones, eyelashes. Insects within and without
had entered through the glass-free windshield of my body,
and in the vertigo of my-self I was alone with my mind.

Among sunshades on a single pole and windshield wipers moved by
    pure chance,
outlandish images beat at my heart. And from the far-off ground,
a dog with a human face watched me as if I were its alter ego.

At the foot of life and death's double pyramid,
the god Quetzalcoatl offered flowers and butterflies
to his followers in place of human flesh.

And amid such splendor, only the sadness was mine.

Self-Portrait at Age Eighty

I never thought I'd spend my eightieth
in a year of plague and populists.
But here I am, confined to my house
in Mexico City, accompanied by Betty,
my wife—all life long,
and by three feral cats that came in off the street;
and oh, by the Virgin of the Apocalypse's image
lit day and night on the stairway wall.

Astral twins, my daughters Chloe and Eva
have turned into my spiritual mothers,
and Josephine, my only grandchild, into a playful grandma.
They are in London and Brooklyn, separated from us,
behind windows, seeing and hearing
the ambulances of death pass by.

Paradises there are that have no country
and my suns are interior suns,
and love—more so than dream—
is a second life,
and I will live it to the last moment
in the tremendous everydayness of the mystery.

Surrounded by light and the warbling of birds,
I live in a state of poetry,
because for me, being and making poetry are the same.
For that I would want, in these final days,
like Titian, to depict the human body one more time.
Dust I shall be, but dust in love.

THE POETS

AMELIA M. GLASER translates primarily from Yiddish, Ukrainian, and Russian. She is Professor of Literature at UC San Diego, where she holds the Chair in Judaic Studies. She is the author of *Jews and Ukrainians in Russia's Literary Borderlands* and *Songs in Dark Times: Yiddish Poetry of Struggle from Scottsboro to Palestine*. She is the editor of *Stories of Khmelnytsky: Competing Literary Legacies of the 1648 Ukrainian Cossack Uprising* and, with Steven S. Lee, *Comintern Aesthetics*. She is currently writing a book about contemporary Ukrainian poetry.

YULIYA ILCHUK is Assistant Professor of Slavic Literature and Culture at Stanford University. She is the author of an award-winning book, *Nikolai Gogol: Performing Hybrid Identity*, and a translator of contemporary Ukrainian poetry. Ilchuk's most recent book project, *The Vanished: Memory, Temporality, Identity in Post-Euromaidan Ukraine*, revisits collective memory and trauma, post-memory, remembrance, memorials, and reconciliation in Ukraine.

HALYNA KRUK was born in Lviv, Ukraine. She is the author of five books of poetry, a collection of short stories, and four children's books. She has garnered multiple awards for her writing, including the Bohdan Ihor Antonych Prize, the Polish Gaude Polonia Fellowship, the BookForum Best Book Award, and the Kovaliv Fund Award for Prose. She has served as vice president of PEN Ukraine, holds a PhD in Ukrainian literature, and is professor of European and Ukrainian baroque literature at the Ivan Franko National University in Lviv.

JORIE GRAHAM was born in New York City, the daughter of a journalist and a sculptor. She was raised in Rome, Italy, and educated in French schools. She studied philosophy at the Sorbonne in Paris before attending New York University as an undergraduate, where she studied filmmaking. She received an MFA in poetry from the University of Iowa. She is the author of fifteen collections of poems. Her poetry has been widely translated and has been the recipient of numerous awards, among them the Pulitzer Prize, the Forward Prize, the *Los Angeles Times* Book Prize, the International Nonino Prize, and the Rebekah Johnson Bobbitt National Prize for Poetry from the Library of Congress. She served as a Chancellor of the Academy of American Poets from 1997 to 2003. She lives in Massachusetts and is currently the Boylston Professor of Rhetoric and Oratory at Harvard University.

ISHION HUTCHINSON was born in Port Antonio, Jamaica. He is the author of the poetry collections *Far District*, which won the PEN/Joyce Osterweil Award for Poetry, and *House of Lords and Commons*, which received the National Book Critics Circle Award for Poetry. He is the recipient of a Guggenheim Fellowship, the Joseph Brodsky Rome Prize in Literature, the Whiting Award, and the Windham-Campbell Prize for Poetry, among other honours.

Poet and essayist ANN LAUTERBACH is the author of eleven books of poetry and three books of essays, including *The Night Sky: Writings on the Poetics of Experience* and *The Given & The Chosen*. Her 2009 collection of poetry, *Or to Begin Again*, was a finalist for the National Book Award. Lauterbach's work has been recognized by fellowships from, among others, the Guggenheim Foundation and the John D. and Catherine T. MacArthur Foundation. She is the Ruth and David Schwab II Professor of Languages and Literatures at Bard College. Born in New York City, she lives in Germantown, New York.

GEORGE MCWHIRTER is an Irish-Canadian writer, translator, editor, teacher, and Vancouver's first Poet Laureate. His first book of poetry,

Catalan Poems, was a joint winner of the first Commonwealth Poetry Prize with Chinua Achebe's *Beware Soul Brother*. He has translated works by Mario Arregui, Carlos Fuentes, and José Emilio Pacheco. He received his MA from the University of British Columbia and stayed on to become a full professor in 1983 and head of the Creative Writing Department from 1983 to 1993. He retired as a Professor Emeritus in 2005. He was made a life member of the League of Canadian Poets in 2005 and is also a member of the Writers' Union of Canada and PEN International. He currently writes full-time and lives in Vancouver, British Columbia.

HOMERO ARIDJIS was born in Contepec, Michoacán, Mexico. He has written fifty-one books of poetry and prose and has won many important literary prizes. Formerly Mexico's ambassador to Switzerland, the Netherlands, and UNESCO, he is also the President Emeritus of PEN International and the founder and president of the Group of 100, an environmentalist association of artists and scientists.

THE JUDGES

ALBERT F. MORITZ was born on April 15, 1947, in Niles, Ohio, USA, and educated at Marquette University, Milwaukee, Wisconsin, from which he received a PhD in eighteenth- and nineteenth-century British poetry. His most recent books of poems are *The Garden: a poem and an essay* (2021), *As Far As You Know* (2020), and *The Sparrow: Selected Poems* (2018). He has published twenty books of poems, and his poetry has received various recognitions, including the Guggenheim Fellowship; inclusion in the Princeton Series of Contemporary Poets; the Ingram Merrill Fellowship; the Award in Literature of the American Academy of Arts and Letters; the Bess Hokin Prize of *Poetry* magazine; the Elizabeth Matchett Stover Award of the *Southwest Review*; the ReLit Award; the Griffin Poetry Prize; the Raymond Souster Award of the League of Canadian Poets; and selection to the Colección Legítima Defensa of the Universidad Autónoma de Zacatecas (Mexico; distinguished foreign authors in translation). He is a three-time finalist for the Governor General's Award for English-language poetry for his books *Rest on the Flight into Egypt* (1999), *The Sentinel* (2008), and *The New Measures* (2012); his book *As Far As You Know* (2020) was a finalist for the Ontario Trillium Book Award. In January 2019 he was selected Poet Laureate of the City of Toronto and served in that role until May 2023.

JAN WAGNER was born in 1971 in Hamburg and has lived in Berlin since 1995. Poet, essayist, translator of anglophone poetry (Charles Simic, James Tate, Margaret Atwood, Ted Hughes, Dylan Thomas,

Simon Armitage, Matthew Sweeney, Robin Robertson, Jo Shapcott, Sujata Bhatt, and many others), he was, until 2003, a co-publisher of the international literature box Die Aussenseite des Elementes ("The Outside of the Element").

Wagner has published eight poetry collections since 2001, most recently *Steine & Erden* (2023) and *Die Live Butterfly Show* (2018). *Regentonnenvariationen* ("*Rain Barrel Variations*"), his sixth collection, won the Leipzig Book Fair Prize in 2015; *Selected Poems 2001–2015* was published in 2016.

Wagner's poetry has been translated into more than forty languages. A selection in English (*Self-Portrait with a Swarm of Bees: Selected Poems*, translated by Iain Galbraith) was published in 2015; another English selection, translated by David Keplinger, came out in 2017 under the title *The Art of Topiary: Selected Poems*. Other books appeared in Italy (*Variazioni sul barile dell'acqua piovana*, 2019), France (*Les Variations de la citerne*, 2019), Sweden, Greece, Poland, Spain, the Netherlands, China, Norway, Serbia, Ukraine, Brazil, Chile, Slovenia, Ukraine, and elsewhere.

Wagner has received various literary awards, among them the Anna Seghers Prize (2004), the Ernst Meister Prize for Poetry (2005), the Friedrich Hölderlin Prize (2011), the Mörike Award (2015), the Leipzig Book Fair Prize (2015), the Zhongkun International Poetry Prize (China, 2017), the Georg Büchner Prize (2017), the Max Jacob Prize (France, 2020), and the PONT International Literary Prize for Intercultural Cooperation (Slovenia, 2021). He is a member of the German Academy for Language and Literature.

Poet, curator, professor, performer, and cultural activist ANNE WALDMAN co-founded the Jack Kerouac School of Disembodied Poetics program at Naropa University. She is the author of over sixty volumes of poetry, poetics, and anthologies, including *The Iovis Trilogy: Colors in The Mechanism of Concealment*, which won the PEN Center Literary Award.

Waldman has read in the streets as well as at numerous larger venues, such as the Dodge Literary Festival in the USA, the Jaipur

Literature Festival in India, and the T. S. Eliot Memorial Foundation at Harvard University. She continues to teach poetics all over the world.

Her album SCIAMACHY was released in 2020 by Fast Speaking Music and the Lévy Gorvy Dayan and has been described by Patti Smith as "exquisitely potent, a psychic shield for our times." Waldman was the keynote speaker for the Dylan and the Beats conference in Tulsa in spring 2022. She wrote the libretto for the critically acclaimed opera/movie *Black Lodge*, featuring music by composer David T. Little, which premiered at Opera Philadelphia in October 2022. *Publishers Weekly* has called Anne Waldman a "counter-cultural giant." Waldman is most recently the author of *Bard, Kinetic* (2023) and co-editor with Emma Gomis of *New Weathers: Poetics from the Naropa Archive* (2022). She is a Chancellor Emeritus of the Academy of American Poets.

ACKNOWLEDGEMENTS

The publisher thanks the following for their kind permission to reprint the work contained in this volume:

"there and back again," "i return on a bus full of quiet children," "God, don't quiet the voice of anger," "mangled blossom," "gray zone," "in this house," "PTSD," and "be honest with yourself" from *A Crash Course in Molotov Cocktails*, by Halyna Kruk, translated by Amelia M. Glaser and Yuliya Ilchuk, are reprinted by permission of Arrowsmith Press.

"Are We," "On the Last Day," "Translation Rain," "They Ask Me," "In Reality," "Can You," "This Vase of Quince Branches You Sent Me," and "Then the Rain," from *To 2040* by Jorie Graham are reprinted by permission of Copper Canyon Press.

Selections from "His Idylls at Happy Grove" ("Agog with corrosive dates …" and "They shovelled the long trenches …"), selections from "The Anabasis of Godspeed" ("XXVIII," "XXX," "XXXI," and "LXIV"), selection from "Three Heroic Emblems" ("Where the sun never conceded …"), and "In Praise of a Shadow" from *School of Instructions* by Ishion Hutchinson are reprinted by permission of Farrar, Straus and Giroux.

"Habitat," "Garden," "Door (*The Said Closes*)," "Alarm," "Door (*And then We Fell*)," "On Relation," "Nocturne," and "Door (*Small Incident*)" from *Door* by Ann Lauterbach are reprinted by permission of Penguin Books.

"Meeting with My Father in the Orchard," "The Sacrificial Stone," "The Sun of the Blind," "Garden of Ghosts," "Poet Beatific," "The Creation of the World by the Animals," "Self-Portrait in the Zone of Silence," and "Self-Portrait at Age Eighty" from *Self-Portrait in the Zone of Silence* by Homero Aridjis, translated by George McWhirter, are reprinted with permission of New Directions.

GRIFFIN POETRY PRIZE ANTHOLOGY 2024

The best books of poetry published in English are honoured each year with the $130,000 Griffin Poetry Prize, one of the world's most prestigious and richest international literary awards. Since 2001 this annual prize has acted as a tremendous spur to interest in and recognition of poetry, focusing worldwide attention on the formidable talent of poets writing in English and works in translation. And each year the editor of the *Griffin Poetry Prize Anthology* gathers the work of the extraordinary poets shortlisted for the award and introduces us to some of the finest poems in their collections.

This year, editor and prize juror Albert F. Moritz's selections from the shortlist include poems from Halyna Kruk's *A Crash Course in Molotov Cocktails*, translated by Amelia M. Glaser and Yuliya Ilchuk (Arrowsmith Press), Jorie Graham's *To 2040* (Copper Canyon Press), Ishion Hutchinson's *School of Instructions* (Farrar, Straus and Giroux), Ann Lauterbach's *Door* (Penguin Books), and Homero Aridjis's *Self-Portrait in the Zone of Silence*, translated by George McWhirter (New Directions).

Judges Albert F. Moritz (Canada), Jan Wagner (Germany), and Anne Waldman (USA) each read 592 books of poetry, including 49 translations from 22 languages, submitted by 235 publishers from 14 different countries.